Russian Blue Cats

by Grace Hansen

abdopublishing.com

Published by Abdo Kids, a division of ABDO, P.O. Box 398166, Minneapolis, Minnesota 55439.

Printed in China

102016

012017

Photo Credits: iStock, Shutterstock, Thinkstock

Production Contributors: Teddy Borth, Jennie Forsberg, Grace Hansen

Design Contributors: Dorothy Toth, Laura Mitchell

Publisher's Cataloging in Publication Data

Names: Hansen, Grace, author.

Title: Russian blue cats / by Grace Hansen.

Description: Minneapolis, Minnesota : Abdo Kids, 2017 | Series: Cats. Set 2 | Includes bibliographical references and index.

Identifiers: LCCN 2016944103 | ISBN 9781680809220 (lib. bdg.) | ISBN 9781680796322 (ebook) | ISBN 9781680796995 (Read-to-me ebook)

Subjects: LCSH: Russian blue cats--Juvenile literature.

Classification: DDC 636.8/2--dc23

LC record available at http://lccn.loc.gov/2016944103

Table of Contents

Russian Blues

Russian Blue cats are known for their silvery blue coats. They are also known for their beautiful green eyes.

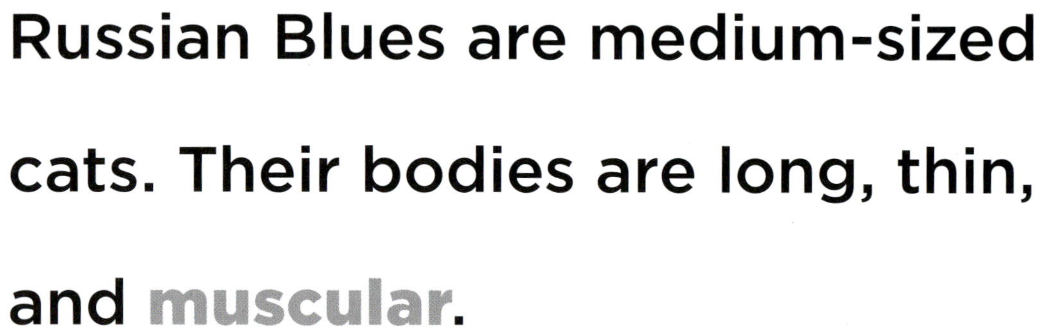

Russian Blues are medium-sized cats. Their bodies are long, thin, and **muscular**.

Russian Blues have large round eyes. Their ears are large, but nicely in **proportion** to the head.

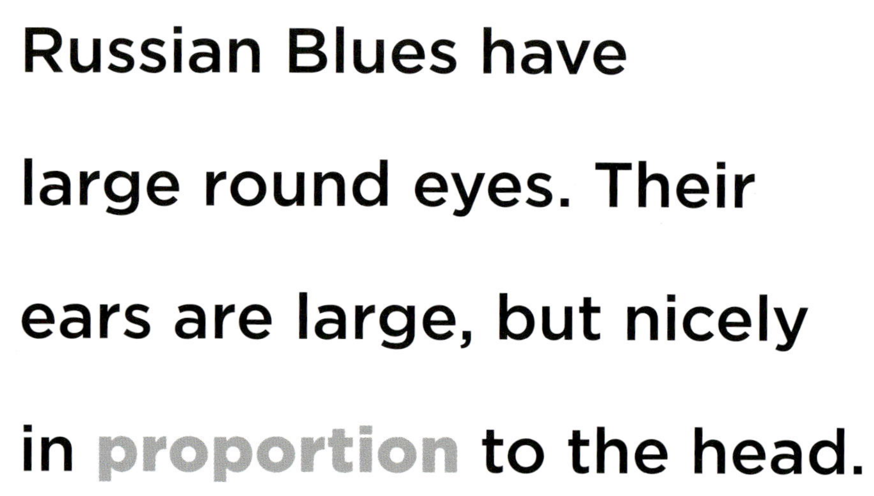

This cat has a beautiful and **plush** coat. It seems as though it shines.

Grooming

Russian Blues do not shed a lot. It is important to brush them weekly to keep the coat healthy.

Personality

Russian Blues are not only known for their beauty. They are also known for their gentle nature.

Russian Blues are loving toward their owners. They like to play fetch. But they are also happy sitting quietly.

Russian Blues do not like changes to their schedules. Feeding them at the same time each day is important.

Russian Blues prefer peace and calm. They do not like **frequent** visitors or loud noises. They are happiest in quiet homes with their families.

More Facts

- Russian Blues are quite **particular** about their litter boxes. They must be kept very, very clean at all times.

- Russian Blues love attention from their owners. But they also do just fine when owners are away at work. This is not usual for intelligent breeds.

- Some Russian Blues have mouths that make them look like they are always smiling.

Glossary

frequent – constant or regular.

muscular – having well-developed muscles.

particular – having very definite opinions about what is acceptable.

plush – thick and soft.

proportion – the relationship between size, shape, and position of an object's different parts.

Index

abdokids.com

Use this code to log on to abdokids.com and access crafts, games, videos and more!